THE ORCHARD

selected stories

Ira Sumner Simmonds

ISS Publishing
Brooklyn, NY

ACKNOWLEDGEMENTS

Thank you to my wife and family, to Verna Richardson and everyone who has supported me in my writing endeavors.

Ira Sumner Simmonds
ISS Publishing
31 Grace Court,
Brooklyn, NY 11201
url: www.irasimmonds.com
email: ira@irasimmonds.com

Cover design and drawings by Boryana Stambolieva

Ordering information:
Available in Print-on-demand and eBook format at Amazon.com and at Barnes & Noble bookstores

THE ORCHARD - selected stories
Copyright © February 2019 by Ira Sumner Simmonds - ISS Publishing

ISBN (Print Edition): 978-0-99987-243-7
ISBN (eBook Edition): 978-0-99987-246-8

AUTHOR'S NOTE

Although my first book, *From Siberia to St. Kitts: A Teacher's Journey* was published in March 2018, my first writing efforts began twenty-eight years earlier in 1991, the year Mother was first diagnosed with early onset Alzheimer's disease.

If we are lucky, we live to see our parents grow old with little or no degradation in their cognitive and physical abilities. If I were to hazard a guess, I would say that most of us are not fully prepared when confronted with the medical, emotional and psychological challenges that beset our elderly parents.

In trying to understand the physiology that was changing Mother's personality, I discovered quite by accident the therapeutic powers of writing. It is however still unclear what precise forces caused me to put pen to paper. Perhaps my unconscious mind recognized that this was the best way for me to deal with my struggle to understand Mother's condition. In short, writing about Mother's illness, putting lots and lots of words on paper, shuffling and reshuffling them until they made sense was not only for me a form of therapy, it also turned me on to the joy of writing.

This book is a compilation of true short stories based on real events written over the past twenty-nine years. In order to maintain their anonymity, pseudonyms were used for the names of all persons mentioned in this anthology.

CONTENTS

Thanks mom - for all of your blessings

Real knowledge is to know the extent of one's ignorance.

—Confucius

CHAPTER 1

The Orchard

About ten years ago Paul had a dream. A big dream. He would build his dream house in Valley Views, a beautiful scenic area in the south eastern foothills of Mount Olivees. Strategically placed on the side of a gently sloping hill, it commanded picturesque panoramic views of the surrounding valleys. The green valleys and rolling hills suggest a fertility of soil unparalleled in any other part of the beautiful Caribbean island of St. Kitts. As your eyes travel leisurely from the top of Mt. Olivees down through the foothills and valleys, the verdant hues, from rainforest green to everything in between, speak eloquently of a bounteous land.

An important feature of Paul's dream was to have an orchard of fruit trees. Many, many different kinds of fruit trees. There would be several varieties of mangoes - grafted, bellyful, rosy cheek, Nevis - as well as

2 • IRA SUMNER SIMMONDS

sugar apple, custard apple, guava, soursop, passion fruit, papaya, banana, and coconut.

Using his incredible multi-faceted skills as a builder, over the course of a few years Paul transformed his dream into reality. As the years went by, the many trees he planted in his orchard matured and soon began to bear fruit. With time, his fruit breakfast options would increased exponentially. And now, five years after he planted his first tree he and his clan live in a kind of fruity paradise, enjoying a delectable array of juicy, pulpy, sugary delights that make him the envy of this land. A land so rich and productive, the indigenous peoples of yore named it Liamigua, or fertile land.

Recently, there has been trouble in paradise. Things did not unfold exactly the way it did in Paul's dream. Oh, the orchard is doing quite well thank you, the trees flourishing in a perfect environment of rich soil and an abundant supply of rainfall. As for the fruit, they get more and more juicy and succulent with each passing year.

For Paul, Valley Views is an idyllic place to live. It is quiet, peaceful and far from the madding crowd. A place where one can observe and enjoy a wide variety of wildlife - red-tail hawks, cattle egrets, sparrows, black swifts, Antillean crested humming birds, mourning doves, purple-throated caribs, yellow warblers, lesser Antillean bullfinches, ground doves, mongooses, monkeys, lizards, to name a few. The sight and sounds of these animals, comingled with the occasional mooing and bleating of domestic cattle, goats and sheep which graze the grassy slopes, give visitors to Valley Views the sense that they are truly in a special place.

Idyllic setting notwithstanding, there is indeed trouble in paradise. Simply put, Paul has a problem. A monkey problem. St. Kitts has an abundance of monkeys and it is said that their numbers far exceed that of the human population. Vervet (or green) monkeys, they are descendants of pets brought to St. Kitts by French colonists in the 1600s.

The Valley Views monkeys were quite cute when they first began to frequent Paul's backyard orchard, but their cuteness quotient would soon fall more precipitously than Wall Street stocks on Black Thursday when the orchard began to produce ripe fruit. And before Paul could say, "Well, I'll be a monkey's uncle", he suddenly recognized the magnitude of his dilemma. Paul did not merely have the proverbial monkey on his back. He had a whole troop of monkeys in his backyard - devouring his delicious various assortment of delicious fruit..

As for the monkeys, it did not take them long to realize that they too had a problem. A Paul problem. They have always operated under the simian assumption that the orchard was rightfully theirs, bequeathed to them by their ancestors through ancient VERVET (**V**alidated to **E**at **R**ipe **V**arieties-of-fruit from **E**very **T**ree) monkey laws. Understanding the significance of these laws, and always wanting to live in peaceful harmony with these vervet monkeys, the early colonists actually bestowed the name of Monkey Hill on the area surrounding Valley Views.

Despite these ancient VERVET monkey laws, a showdown between Paul and the monkeys seemed inevitable. The monkeys wanted, or rather, demanded unlimited access to the orchard. Paul, on the other hand, was determined to deny them free access to *his* backyard bounty. Now, Paul is not at all an unreasonable guy. He agreed in principle with the loose terms of the **V**alidated to **E**at **R**ipe **V**arieties-of-fruit from **E**very **T**ree law and was perfectly willing to share the fruits of his labor. However, the concept of sharing was totally lost on the monkeys. Particularly unacceptable was their wasteful bite-and-drop habit. They would pick a fruit, take a bite or two then discard it.

Much to Paul's chagrin the war for control of the orchard became a protracted one. For weeks the monkeys came, ate to their hearts' desire, littering the orchard with an assortment of half-eaten fruit. With their smarts, agility, quickness and stealth, they somehow possess a special knack for knowing when fruit is ripe, arriving and helping themselves before Paul, or the birds (welcome melodious-voiced invités to the orchard), knew that there was ripe fruit to be had.

Needless to say, Paul was not pleased. The monkey raiders were putting a serious dent in his plans for a daily breakfast of fruit. It was time to devise a plan of action. The monkeys, led by a large alpha male, were getting bolder by each day. They could now be regularly seen sitting jauntily on the back veranda's railing. The alpha male, a large menacing specimen, was something to behold. He sported a nervous tic. Paul named him Ticky, the involuntary spasm of the head serving to imbue him with a thuggish persona. Sure would not like to meet him alone in a dark alley, Paul thought. A fearless warrior, on occasion Ticky could be seen peeking into the house through the rear windows overlooking the orchard, casing the joint perhaps, an advance reconnaissance special forces raider gathering intel for a grand monkey plot to break into Paul's house and steal (or rather, take back) all the fruit that Paul had illegally obtained from *their* orchard. After all, did Paul not read the special clause of the Vervet Monkey Law which says that monkeys have exclusive rights to **all** fruit cultivated, produced, found in (or transported to) any area within a five-mile radius of Monkey Hill? Googling Vervet Monkey Law, Paul discovered that there was indeed such a law. However, contrary to claims made by the monkeys, Paul also discovered that the provisions under this law did **not** cover **all** fruit. Only bananas.

With the situation getting out of hand, Paul was forced to think of ways to protect his property from these marauding bandits. Perhaps he should electrify the orchard fence. Not with enough voltage to electrocute these simian raiders, but just enough to give them a mild shock that would deter them from entering the orchard. Not a bad idea, Paul thought, but one that, given the necessary investment in materials and time, must be shelved for a plan that could be implemented immediately, before all the fruit was stolen. Such was the urgency to find a solution to the monkey problem.

Perhaps he can build a trap and try to catch a monkey, keep it on display in the orchard for a few days so that other monkeys may bear witness to the fate of trespassers. Not having ever studied the behavioral habits of the feral vervet monkeys of St. Kitts, Paul could not really predict how they would react to being trapped as a means of deterring the daily raids on his orchard. Intuitively, he knew that he was dealing with highly intelligent creatures. He did not (not even for a moment) labor under the delusion that he, in any form or fashion, would have the upper hand in a long protracted war against the monkeys. He knew, somehow, that the task of ridding his orchard of monkeys would be a daunting one. They were much too smart, plus they had the crucial advantage of time. They can simply outwait him. They knew that he could not very well stand guard over 'his' precious orchard twenty-four seven. They knew this because, hidden from view in the neighboring trees beyond the fence of the orchard, they could see Paul and his clan leave for work and school every morning between the hours of 7:30 and 8:30. Paul in a white SUV, his wife and son in a grey van. Occasionally, in an attempt to confuse the monkeys, Paul would don his helmet and leave for work on his motor scooter.

Paul reasoned, having consulted with his friends and colleagues who have had a wide array of 'monkey' experiences, that a monkey trapped in his orchard would be a deterrent to other monkey raiders. Presumably they would see one of their own lose its freedom and decide, at an emergency monkey community meeting, that even though Paul's bananas (or *their* bananas, if you side with the monkeys) were the most succulent on the island, the risk would be too great. They would then remove the Valley Views Orchard from their list of daily foraging stops. The more Paul mulled over the idea of catching a monkey, the more he became convinced that doing so would produce favorable results. But it also meant that he would have to find the time to build a trap.

Perhaps he could put his recently-acquired field archery skills to good use, using the monkey marauders for target practice. If only he could just scare them into thinking that *his* orchard was not a safe place to forage. Will a direct hit with one of his target practice arrows give them pause? He could not be sure but after reflecting on this idea for a few days, he decided that it was an idea worth trying.

His opportunity came one Saturday afternoon when, from the kitchen window, his glance fell upon a monkey heading in the direction of the papaya tree. He quickly went downstairs, retrieved his bow and arrows and ran back upstairs to his bathroom, the area of the house closest to the papaya tree. He should be able to get off at least one good shot from point-blank range with the papaya tree not more than five feet from the bathroom windows. That's all he would need. One good shot. Trying his best not to be seen, Paul flattened himself against the wall on the right side of the closest window. Even though the glazed slightly tinted panes were closed, he still had to be cautious, not wanting to chance spooking the monkey with his shadowy silhouette. The sound of his pounding heart echoed in his ears. There was a sudden rustling noise on the other side of the window. Paul froze. He wondered if the raucous din caused by his pounding heart alerted his prey to the hidden danger lurking behind the bathroom wall. Still leaning against the wall Paul began to turn, in super-slow motion, the window crank.

After what felt like an eternity a grayish-green fur coat slowly, like a darkroom-developed photograph, came into view. It was the Alpha male in all his splendor. A few more turns of the crank and the picture was fully developed. Ticky, framed in papaya-eating profile by the 2" by 15" inch oblong opening between two eye-level glazed panes. This close, he was even more awesome. So impressively fit and big was Ticky that Paul could not help but admire him, happy to be doing so, however, from the relative safety of his bathroom. Observing this wily creature more carefully, Paul marveled at the dexterous efficiency with which Ticky was dispatching the reddish yellow papaya held delicately with both hands.

As Paul admired Ticky, he flashed on a monkey story recently told to him by a friend. She claimed that one day she decided to drive her three young kids out to the Southeast Peninsula for lunch at the Reggae Beach Bar & Grill. A few minutes after turning onto a dusty dirt road she saw a troop of monkeys up ahead. Slowing down to a crawl, she came to within fifty-feet of the troop before coming to a full stop. The troop had not given way. Just as she was trying to decide what to do, the biggest member of the troop (she thought it might have been the alpha male), took three steps in her direction, stopped, raised himself on his hind legs and, moving his head from side to side (as if assessing the danger), glared at the car. She swore that by using his back legs to elevate himself, he was as tall as she was. Frightened, she ordered her kids to roll up the windows, slammed the car in reverse and sped backwards towards the safety of the paved road.

But this was not the time for flashbacks or for paying homage to this handsome bandit. This was the time to teach Ticky and his clan a valuable lesson on the perils of trespassing. Suddenly realizing that he would lose this monkey lesson-teaching moment if he did not act quickly, Paul grabbed his bow. In one smooth motion he placed the aluminum arrow on the arrow rest, the feathered end nestling against the bowstring. He must act quickly and quietly. His back still against the wall, he pulled on the bowstring. Trying his best not to hit the glass pane, he inserted the aluminum arrow through the two-inch opening between panes. The arrow trembled slightly as the tension of the bowstring on his biceps, combined with the pounding in his chest made it difficult to keep it steady. Ping! The arrow hit the glass before Paul could take aim. Ticky, alert as ever, turned his head sharply. Paul held his breath, expecting Ticky to disappear in a flash. Instead, and much to Paul's surprise, Ticky stood on his hind legs and turned to face the window. With his flat, black face set in an hourglass-shaped fringe of yellowish gray fur and his light-brown eyes that exuded supreme confidence, he was truly the master of his domain. For a second or two, time stood still as Paul and Ticky (his nervous tic now gone) stared at each other in frozen silence, each in his own way startled by the other. Ticky, by the surprising sight and proximity of Paul pointing a thin stick at him, and Paul, by Ticky's fearless confrontational stance. What's with the stick? And why was he pointing it at me? Ticky seemed to be thinking. Paul, on the other hand was wondering why Ticky didn't immediately flee.

Muscles aching Paul pulled the bowstring all the way back and released the arrow. Ticky let out a loud scream and fell from the papaya tree. Almost as soon as he hit the ground three troop members were quickly at his side. Helped by his three compadres, Ticky hopped over the fence, the arrow still stuck in him.

In the ensuing four weeks not a monkey was to be seen in the orchard. Was this the end of the raids? Paul had a feeling that it was only a matter of time before they returned.

And return they did. Not the Ticky troop, but a new and smaller group comprised of a large male, a mature female with a newborn baby and a juvenile female. How did this troop (Paul named it the Kool troop in honor of the mature female's cool and unflappable demeanor) inherit such a coveted fruit-laden territory? Did this Kool troop simply fill the vacuum created by the disappearance of the Ticky troop or was the acquisition of this territory the result of the Kool troop's alpha male winning it in battle? Paul wondered what happened to the Ticky troop. Was Ticky seriously injured? Did he die? Did he survive the hit and decide to establish territory elsewhere where it was less dangerous? If he did die, what happened to the other members of his troop? Did they join another troop? Lots of questions but very few answers. Paul wished he could devote time to the study of these fascinating creatures.

It was now time to implement the next anti-monkey-trespassing plan. A few days later and Paul was ready to try out his recently built 5' x 4' x 6' wood and wire mesh trap cage. The mechanism that sprung the trap was simple. When a monkey enters the cage and pulls on the fruit, a string attached to the fruit lure releases the 'spring' causing the trap door of the cage to fall. The trap, armed with ripe bananas was now set. Two uneventful weeks went by. Paul, thinking that the trap was set too close to the house, decided to move it as far away from the house as possible, placing it close to the back fence in the furthest part of the orchard. Another two uneventful weeks went by. It wasn't that the orchard was absent of monkeys. They could be seen visiting the orchard every morning. But how could they resist the temptation of the mouth-watering yellow bananas in the cage? Easily, it turned out. It wasn't long before Paul realized that the monkeys had options. There were equally delicious bananas in the trees. And given a choice between climbing a banana tree and entering a wire-meshed cage to get a banana, a wild monkey will always choose the climbing option. Shucks, these monkeys always seem to be one step ahead of me, Paul thought. He decided to harvest the remaining ripe bananas before the monkeys ate them all. Three days went by and the bananas were still in the cage, untouched. The bananas placed on the ground outside the cage as an enticement to enter the cage were a different matter. Each morning members of the Kool troop could be seen sitting near the cage leisurely enjoying a breakfast of bananas.

Three more days went by but the bananas in the cage remained undisturbed while those placed on the ground in front of the cage's trap door continued to disappear. Paul was at a loss to figure out why they weren't entering the cage. Suddenly it hit him. Removing ripe bananas from the trees and placing them on the ground to entice the monkeys to enter the cage was not a workable strategy because the concept of enticement was probably another one of those things lost on the monkeys. Monkey sees banana, monkey eats banana - providing of course that the banana is in its natural setting, like in a tree or on the ground. Not that they won't enter your house or a baited cage to get a banana. They certainly would and sometimes do, but only as a means of last resort. In desperate times when food is scarce a monkey would do desperate things to get food. For now, there was no need to enter the wire mesh cage with the board floor because at the Valley Views orchard there was a variety of available fruit. You could pick them from a tree or, thanks to Paul, you could pick them up from the ground.

Paul was impressed with the remarkable self-restraint exhibited by these monkeys. Meanwhile, the cost in bananas of trying to trap a monkey kept mounting as Kool troop was fast becoming the best fed monkeys in St. Kitts. Paul wondered if by 'feeding' these monkeys he was exacerbating his monkey problem. Was he in effect advertising to the monkey community that the Valley Views orchard was *the* place to get free fruit? Paul was afraid that this might be the inevitable and unintended outcome of his efforts to catch a monkey. Although he probably would not admit it, his frustration at not being able to nab one was slowly building. To make matters worse, two days ago his wife insinuated that fruit she recently purchased from the market mysteriously disappeared, used, she is certain, in Paul's monkey-catching endeavors. Not wanting to incriminate himself, Paul refused to respond to her veiled accusation.

Change of strategy. It was time for a more no-nonsense approach. The free bananas era was over. Paul made certain that the only ripe bananas available to the monkeys would be those in the cage attached to the trap mechanism. Four days went by and the bunch of bananas in the cage was still untouched. On the fifth day all the bananas disappeared. How was it possible to remove the bananas from the bunch without activating the trap door? There was only one way to solve this mystery. Taking a page out of zoologist Jane Goodall's book, Paul decided to find some time in his busy schedule to just sit and observe the Kool troop. The next day he went downstairs to his den at 6:45 AM, turned off the lights and sat at the window which best afforded him an unobstructed view of the banana-baited cage, strategically placed close to the fence at the far end of the orchard. From where he sat he had a good view of the tall trees that lined the far fence of the orchard. The branches of these trees act as a sort of monkey highway. Paul can usually tell when a troop is approaching by the manner in which the branches undulated. Sort of like the human wave you see at Yankee Stadium when fans try to rally the team, or the advancing waves of the nearby Atlantic Ocean on a stormy day.

At 7:06 am the rhythmic movement of the branches signaled the troop's arrival. A minute later a monkey was in the orchard walking towards the cage. Without hesitation, it entered, took a banana from the bunch, exited the cage, sat with his back against a palm tree and began to peel and eat the banana. Paul was flabbergasted. He had tested and retested the trap's trip mechanism beforehand and it worked perfectly each time. Paul, a great problem-solver, looked on admiringly at this crafty banana-eating critter, wracking his brains as he tried to figure out why the door release failed to activate. Meanwhile the monkey finished eating the banana, got up, strolled into the trap once again, took another banana and returned to his eating position next to the palm tree. Paul readied his binoculars. If the monkey returned for a third banana he would get a close-up look and perhaps figure out why the trap door twice failed to activate. When the monkey returned to the cage to get its third banana the binoculars were already focused, trained on the bunch of bananas. As it did before, the monkey entered the trap, casually picked a banana and immediately exited the trap. Holding the uneaten banana in its left hand, it scaled the fence and disappeared into the trees.

It took a few seconds for Paul to fully process what he had just witnessed. Then, suddenly, it all made sense. Paul designed the trap so that in the act of *pulling* a banana from the bunch, the monkey would exert enough tension on the trip line to release the trap door. Instead of *pulling* however, the monkey simply *twisted* the ripe banana from the bunch, exerting little or no tension on the trip line. Had Paul known that wild monkeys twisted rather that pulled bananas from the bunch he would have designed the trap differently. Paul wondered how much monkey-behavior knowledge he needed before he became enlightened enough to catch a monkey. This last trespasser appeared to be a juvenile. Why did the other members of the troop not enter the orchard, choosing instead to wait in the trees outside the fence? Was this juvenile sent into harm's way because it was the lowest ranking member of the troop and therefore expendable? Paul wished he knew more about these fascinating creatures but, for the moment, he needed to devise a new plan.

The quickest and easiest method would be to observe the monkey enter the cage and manually pull the trap door release. And so, after monkeying around with the trip mechanism, modifications to the trap were in place. Paul awoke early the following morning ready to catch a monkey. The day before, he had attached a very long string to the cage's trap door release and extended it across the length of the orchard through the trees and in through the downstairs rec room window. From here he would be able to see the monkey enter the cage and activate the trap door with a quick tug of the string.

Paul did not have to wait long before the undulating branches signaled the troop's arrival. Like clockwork, they were now arriving daily at the orchard between 7:00 and 7:20 am. A monkey (it appeared to be the juvenile female) was now in the orchard ambling towards the cage. Grabbing the string, Paul was now ready to catch his first monkey. Into the cage she went. Just before she reached the bananas positioned at the back of the cage, Paul pulled the string. Hearing the thud of the trapdoor, she stopped, turned and walked (much too casually, Paul thought, given her suddenly imprisoned status) towards the closed door. Reaching out with her right hand she touched the wooden door, turned and walked back to the bananas, sat down, picked a banana, peeled it and began eating. After consuming the banana, she walked to the cage's entrance, touched the closed door one more time before returning to consume, quite leisurely, two more bananas. Captivity is inconsequential when trapped with a bunch of delicious ripe bananas. Sated, she got up and began in earnest to investigate the seriousness of her dilemma. Pacing from one end of the trap to the next she pawed at the sides of the cage looking for a way out. Not finding a breach she sat in the middle of the cage and looked about her pensively as if contemplating a strategy for liberating herself. Paul thought that she was remarkably calm for a trapped animal and wondered why she was not in a state of panic. Was she waiting to be set free by members of her troop? Did they know she was trapped? Why wasn't she screaming?

Monkeys have a variety of vocalizations, each with its own unique significance, but this monkey had not uttered one sound since the trap door fell. And even though Paul could neither see nor hear any other member of the troop, he suspected that they were quietly hiding and observing the drama from the trees beyond the orchard's fence. Curious to see her reaction when approached, Paul exited the house and strolled towards the caged monkey. As soon as she saw Paul she immediately tried to flee and ran headlong into the wire mesh. As Paul drew closer she began, for the first time, to emit high-pitched calls. The response from troop members in the trees was immediate. Suddenly Paul could see them jumping around on the outer branches. They were soon screaming and lunging threateningly at him from above. Feeling that at any moment they might leap from the branches into the orchard to attack him, Paul picked up a stick from the ground, just in case. The screaming stopped when Paul retreated to the house.

Paul fed and observed the trapped juvenile female for two days. During this time no other monkey entered the orchard, but whenever he went near the cage they would appear instantly, hooting and hollering from the trees outside the fence. Paul was truly impressed with the Kool troop's display of loyalty to the trapped juvenile. Their refusal to abandon a trapped member of their kin spoke volumes for their sense of family and community.

Would the drama of the trapped juvenile now deter monkeys from raiding his fruit trees? The answer? An emphatic NO. The very next day after the juvenile's release they were back looking for fruit. Paul immediately put another bunch of ripe bananas in the trap to see what lessons they had learned. Would they now avoid the cage at all costs? Monkeys must have very short memories. Either that or delicious ripe bananas induce in monkeys a temporary state of amnesia, because the next day Paul caught the mature female with her infant clinging to her chest. She casually walked into the cage as though it was a familiar haunt, sat down and began eating bananas. She did not even flinch when the trap door fell, discovering she was trapped only after she had eaten three bananas and was ready to leave the cage. The troop did their usual barking and screaming at Paul from the trees outside the fence while the captive mother was as amazingly poised as a trapped wild creature could possibly be. She held her baby closer to her chest when Paul approached, turning her back as if to hide it, or perhaps to thwart any kidnapping attempts. All this she did without histrionics or any visible exhibition of fear. She was so calm she even took bananas and other fruit right out of Paul's hand. It was as if she instinctively willed herself to be calm in the face of danger and, in so doing, activating maternally-protective pheromones to be absorbed by her vulnerable baby as a protection against stress. Paul liked her style and was totally impressed with this rather cool monkey mother. The next day he set her free.

For the next few months nary a monkey was seen in the orchard. Although Paul could not be sure if their disappearance was positively linked to his efforts, he was convinced, somehow, that all this monkey business was now finally behind him. At first glance he appeared quite pleased with the idea of not seeing another monkey ever again in his orchard. I suspect, however, that Paul secretly misses the visits of this troop of monkeys to his orchard.

CHAPTER 2

Jeremy

N o one has ever explained how I got my name. Not that I have ever
tried to find out, because, truth be told, it doesn't really matter.
What matters is that I've had a good life.

My name is Jeremy and I am a Brooklyn Heights Retriever. No need
to rush to verify with Mr. Google whether or not such a breed of dog exists.
Suffice it to say that you will not find it on the American Kennel Club's list
of dog breeds. Be that as it may, whenever anyone questions my owners
about my breed, that's what they say. I love my adoptive parents dearly and
I really don't think they would fib about such an important thing.

I never really got to know my birth parents but from what I've gathered, I was born at the SUNY Downstate Medical School in Brooklyn in
1963. Someone had the bright idea to attempt to discover if a bitch can
carry healthy puppies to term after having had her stomach removed. I
won't bore you with the details. The answer is yes. My mother gave birth

to a litter of healthy pups. At eight weeks old, I was adopted by Dr. Francis and his family who live in Brooklyn Heights.

Over the years I've heard it murmured *sotto voce* that I am really just a mutt. I am quite proud of this moniker because Dr. Francis and his family are quite knowledgeable and they constantly recount tales of my canine smarts. I love them dearly. In their household I am treated like a king.

Interestingly, Dr. Francis likes to say that *a man must never be a slave to his dog.* I hear him say this constantly to his wife and daughters, and to anyone else who cares to listen. But although Dr. Francis thinks I'm smart, the fact of the matter is that I am not smart enough to know what exactly this saying means. I am after all just a dog. One thing I do know, is that I love to chew on bones. Yes indeed, I love me some bones. Not just any type of bones mind you, I frequently spend hours, days or sometimes weeks trying to get the marrow out of a lamb bone. Dr. Francis, not liking to see me fight with my bones, usually ends up dislodging the tasty marrow for me with a skewer.

I also love grapes. Boy, do I love grapes! An odd thing for a dog to like, you might say. But yes, I am a grape-loving dog. Eating grapes however, poses quite a problem. Without failure, the skin never fails to get stuck somewhere in my mouth. Sometimes life is so difficult for us dogs. Looking at me try to dislodge grape skin stuck between my teeth is not a pretty sight. Dr. Francis is the best owner a dog could ever have. He has recently taken to peeling and pitting my grapes for me. He says it's too painful to watch the convulsive contortions of my lips, tongue, cheeks and face. You humans, blessed with your apposable thumbs, have it so easy. I could continue with other examples of Dr. Francis not being a slave to his dog but I think you get the picture.

I really don't remember much about my early days of adoption with the Francis family. This is understandable given that I was only eight weeks old when I first entered his home. He tells his friends that house-breaking me was a snap. To this very day I still get kudos for my early mastery of the art of not peeing and pooing on the rugs. Dr. Francis and his family still tell stories about how quickly I learned that the only proper place for me to do my business is outside. And not just anywhere outside mind you. I was trained to go, not on the sidewalk but in the gutter. For reasons beyond my ability to comprehend, humans do not like to be greeted with the sight and smells of doggie pee and doggie poo upon leaving or entering their homes. This is one of the major differences between dogs and humans. We can *go* anywhere. Don't get me wrong, I'm not complaining about the fact that my human family gets to take care of its business inside while I'm obliged to do mine outside. Au contraire, I am quite happy with this arrangement. For one, it gives me a chance to stretch my legs a bit. I say 'a bit' as there isn't really much leg-stretching I can do while attached to a leash, but such is the life of a dog. Nevertheless, I do enjoy being *taken out* - not just because I have urgent *business* to attend to, but also because I have other important things to do - like the business of covering up the urine scent of other neighborhood dogs whose single-minded purpose is to cover up *my* most recent scent marks. You'd be surprised to learn how many dogs have come by and peed over my scent marks since the last time I was outside, less than twenty-four hours ago. With all those scent marks to revisit, it's tedious work and not a great deal of time in which to get it done. For once in my lifetime I would love to be able to cover them all.

One of my most favorite things to do during the summer with my adoptive parents is to go sailing. We would all pile into the station wagon and Dr. Francis would drive us out to the Mirage Boat Club in Sheepshead Bay where his Ensign sailboat *Olokon* is moored. We would have so much fun sailing out into the bay, often sailing past Manhattan and Coney Island beaches.

Did I mention that going sailing with Dr. Francis is a real blast? The strangest thing happens to me whenever I discover that we are going sailing. From the moment I see Dr. Francis go to the basement and start pulling out the sailing paraphernalia, the jib, the rudder, the lines, etc., I simply go nuts with excitement, racing up and down the stairs, all around the house barking, jumping, spinning like a mad dog. I literally turn into Pavlov's dog, my animated and frenetic conditioned response triggered by the sight and smell of the sailing gear. Even before we get into the station wagon to drive to the boat club, I could feel the wonderful sensation of the salty air filling my lungs as I point my nose into the wind. I've been known to jump out the window of the station wagon in front of the marina and go sit outside the gate of the boat club impatiently waiting for Dr. Francis to return from parking the car. I get so excited that I'm usually the first one to jump from the dock to the tender and the first one to hop from the tender to *Olokon*. I'm also usually the first one (in fact the only one) to throw up as soon as *Olokon* leaves the mooring. I have a sensitive stomach, what can I say.

The event that usually marks the first day of summer in our house-hold is that day in late June or early July when Dr. Francis sails the Ensign down from its winter marina in Mill Basin to the Mirage Boat Club in Sheepshead Bay.

Sailing with Dr. Francis and his family is always an adventure. One year, at the beginning of the sailing season, one of his daughters and I accompanied him and his wife to Mill Basin in order to bring down the boat. It was a beautiful sunny day. In the words of Dr. Francis, "a great day for sailing." I cannot really call myself a sailor, but I do love sailing with Dr. Francis. I love being on the ocean about as much as I love chas-ing seagulls.

As usual, as soon as we left the mooring I emptied the contents of my stomach on the floor of the cockpit. I have no idea why this happens. Not to worry. My family, aware of my propensity to barf at the outset of every sail-ing trip, is always prepared. In two shakes of a dog's tail it's all cleaned up.

Dr. Francis is not only my best friend, he's also a great sailor, a great captain and one who runs a tight ship, um.... tight boat. He expects his orders to be executed *toute suite* because in the sailing community, it is important to *look good on the water*. If the crew does not respond quickly, the boat might go into irons. My limited understanding of English notwithstanding, when Dr. Francis *barks* the commands to *hard alee; let out the jib; trim the sails*, I usually rush to help, occasionally tripping up another member of the crew.

I have always been impressed with Dr. Francis' navigational skills. Because I'm a dog, I can never be certain that my understanding of the English language is spot on, but I'm pretty certain that I've heard it said that during the Second World War he was an officer in the U. S. Navy.

Dr. Francis took the helm as we sailed South from the East Horse Basin marina, then tacked East under the Belt Parkway into Horse Basin. Half an hour later we were heading South into Jamaica Bay, passing Floyd Bennett Field and the U. S. Marine Corps Center on the right. The tide was rising and there was an urgency, a race against time to get to the Marine Parkway Bridge, a vertical-lift bridge which spans the Rockaway Inlet, connecting the Rockaway Peninsula with the Marine Park area of Brooklyn. Dr. Francis explained that we would lose a lot of time getting to the boat club in Sheepshead Bay if when we got to the bridge the tide was too high for us to pass. He would rather not have to have to stop and wait for the bridge to be raised.

When we got to the bridge it was decided that the window of opportunity for passing under was small but not closed. Dr. Francis blew the air horn to signal that we were coming through and the bridge operator signaled us on. Midway under the bridge there was a clang and a jolt as the top of the mast got caught in the metal grating of the bridge.

I cannot speak for other dogs but it is quite unnerving to see my master and other members of his family come undone. It's true what they say about us. We do have the ability to smell fear, indeed the ability to discern even the slightest of apprehensions in the humans who feed, walk and pamper us. Everyone on the boat got extremely quiet at the realization that the mast was stuck under the bridge. Everyone, that is, except for me. Don't know why but my natural reaction to such situations is to make a lot of noise. The pleas for me to be quiet only caused me to bark even louder and become even more frantic. A lot of frantic barking usually helps in these situations.

The bridge-keeper, aware that we were trapped under the bridge, had the presence of mind to quickly lower the traffic bars, stopping both train and vehicular traffic in both directions. He shouted down to Dr. Francis to turn on the outboard motor and try to power through the problem while he simultaneously pushed the top of the mast down from between the roadway metal grating. When that did dislodge the boat, he tied a rope to the top of the mast and enlisted the help of a motorboat in the area to pull the top of the mast down. Through it all, I kept running from bow to stern barking as loudly as I could. Humans refer to this kind of behavior as freaking out. The steeper *Olokon* was tilted and the closer we came to being tossed overboard, the more frenetically I barked. After a few minutes, somehow the tilted boat, with its mast at an almost ninety-degree angle, suddenly popped free of the bridge and we came out on the other side. The sudden motion of the mast swinging back to an upright position was so scary that I went absolutely nuts for another few minutes before I realized that we were no longer stuck and had emerged safely under the bridge.

Dr. Francis skillfully came about and maneuvered *Olokon* into the wind as two squawking seagulls soared above. Soon the mainsail was pregnant with a wind that blew away all anxieties of pending disaster. A straight tack two nautical miles due North West and an hour later we were securing *Olokon* to its mooring at the Mirage Boat Club.

CHAPTER 3

Backyard Overture

I t was one of those perfect summer days on Martha's Vineyard. The skies were sunny and blue with soft fluffy cumulus clouds lazily floating by. The temperature hovered around a comfortable 80 degrees and a cool northerly breeze rustled the leaves of the backyard trees.

The rented summerhouse in Katama seemed light years away from my Manhattan apartment. A bucolic setting, where the phones did not ring and the beach was a mere ten-minute bike ride away. This would be the first opportunity all year to unwind, recuperate, reevaluate, reflect and be reenergized after completing my first year as a middle school administrator and elementary school summer program supervisor. From inside I could hear the joyful singing of a multi-voiced avian orchestra. An ode to the weather gods who had blessed us with perfect weather. Perfect spirit-lifting weather, made more perfect in the context of the recent dreary rain-filled weeks of July.

I gazed lazily out the kitchen window in search of this avian concert. The backyard feeder appeared to be the concert stage. Fascinated by the music of this ragtag band of musicians, I decided to find a seat, preferably in the front row, a place where I could observe the performers up close. With my book in hand I headed for the chaise lounge nestled in a corner of the backyard close to a tall, thick pine tree about 20 feet from the bird-feeder. There was no other way to get to my seat without disturbing the per-formance - and there would be no break after the first movement to allow latecomers to take their seats. I will do my very best to make my way to my seat without disturbing the concert. Sure enough, as I opened the back door there was a loud flutter of birds on the wing as they scattered to the shelter of nearby trees. Perhaps if I sit quietly they will eventually forgive my lack of concert etiquette and return to the stage to resume the concert. A few minutes later, like starving musicians motivated by the availability of free food, one by one they began to return to the feeder.

Before long I was being treated to a cacophonous yet pleasant sym-phony as these winged musicians competed for a position at the backyard feeder. At first glance, or rather at first listen (the great variety of birds made it a visual and auditory treat), the stage for this performance appeared to be the birdfeeder. I soon realized that there were various songs and calls emanating from many hidden tree perches in the backyard. It was a sort of virtual concert with the birdfeeder as center stage and offstage musicians on hidden perches echoing and mimicking themes and motifs, creating the illusion of surround sound.

The music contractor assembled a truly multi-genus group of musi-cians. Not being an experienced birder, I was unable to identify all of the tunes and calls that reached my ears. However, from those who did make an appearance center stage, on the picket fence, on the ground - with the help of my *Field Guide to the Birds of North America*, I was able to spot black-capped chickadees, northern cardinals, blue jays, wood thrushes, house sparrows, chipping sparrows, mourning doves, house finches, warblers and Arcadian flycatchers.

It suddenly occurred to me after ten minutes of listening and observing that this was perhaps not really a concert but a jam session. Perhaps it was the way in which the musicians entered and left the stage. From time to time different players would come and go as they periodically replaced each other. Fights broke out sporadically over the right to be center stage at the feeder. There were those, like the bossy blue jays, who had total access while others had to await their turn or steal an opportunity to be at the feeder. There seemed to be a hierarchical system in place that determined the comings and goings of each genus of musician. And throughout the entire performance I could hear the background music of several shy musicians who never managed to make a visual appearance. Only two of these instruments were recognizable to me - the doleful cooing of mourning doves and the unmistakable hooting of an owl.

Suddenly, two adult female northern cardinals landed on the ground below the feeder and began feeding on seeds that fell from the tumultuous birdfeeder above. With their reddish-brown crests and wings, and their stately bearing, they seemed out of place retrieving seeds from the ground. As they cocked their heads, looking disdainfully down their distinctive yellow beaks, they were imbued with an aura which signaled that they were too sophisticated to participate in the wild jam session of the hoi polloi at the feeder above.

I was soon distracted by a gray squirrel who joined the cardinals feeding on the ground. Half way up the birdfeeder pole was an upside-down metal bowl strategically placed to deter marauding squirrels from raiding the feeder. I wondered whether or not it had ever tried to scale the pole. Today however, there was no need to as there were lots of pickings on the ground. Squirrels are such wily, agile and intelligent creatures - true masters of their domain. Like Chinese acrobats and well-trained, finely-tuned athletes they move about from ground to tree top with gravity-defying ease and an economy of motion that is unparalleled in the animal kingdom. He did not even glance up to consider the bounty of seeds and grain suspended above him. He meticulously stuck his head in the grass, picked up the seeds with his front paws, sat on his haunches so that he can have a 360-degree view of his surroundings (a survival technique that makes it just about impossible to sneak up on a squirrel) and nibbled. As I marveled at his eating efficiency and his economy of movement, I wondered if he was enjoying the backyard overture played by this rag tag band. Seemingly in response to my musings about his taste in music, he flicked his tail, picked up a few more seeds and continued gnawing.

I was studying his furtive foraging movements when there was a sudden and loud roar of fluttering wings. In a flash, all of the musicians had disappeared into the shelter of the nearby trees and bushes. There was not a bird in sight. A deafening silence followed. It was as though someone had pulled the plug on the concert. It reminded me of a summer night in the late seventies. I was on the Promenade at Avery Fisher Hall working a Boz Skaggs concert when the music suddenly stopped. The city had experienced a blackout that crippled it for almost 24 hours. Even the self-confident squirrel had vanished. Something must have spooked them, I thought. A few seconds later I looked up and saw a red tail hawk circling above the backyard.

It took another ten minutes after the hawk disappeared before everyone was relaxed enough to return to the stage. I was still contemplating the recent hawk drama when I saw my squirrel dashing across the upper branches of the neighbor's tree. He made a sharp left turn on a branch overhanging the house, took a flying leap over the picket fence and landed on the roof. In hot pursuit came a young Siamese cat (probably the neighbor's) flying over the picket fence, landing on the picnic table next to the house. She appeared to have had some notion of catching herself a squirrel. Her gaze was fixed on the roof of the house for at least four minutes, her tail flicking back and forth in excited anticipation of a catch. But the squirrel had long disappeared.

Finally losing interest in the squirrel, she decided to creep under the low-lying branches of the nearby pine tree. Her flicking tail and twitching ears suggested that she was quite pissed at her failure to land the squirrel. She seemed determined to ambush something, any living thing that she can get her claws into. As I sat on my chaise lounge watching this backyard drama unfold, it occurred to me that she was unaware of my presence. I decided not to draw attention to myself. I should allow her to discover me, I thought. I felt myself exhale and realized for the first time that I had been holding my breath. In my effort not to disturb the concert (again) and with all this drama, I had remained in the same position - legs crossed, my book opened on my knees. Upon further consideration, maybe this was neither a concert nor a jam session but an opera. There were certainly enough dramatic twists and turns (not to mention life and death scenes) to please any Puccini aficionado.

Things were soon back to normal as, slowly but surely, the birds began to sing and call to each other and once again began to jostle for position on the feeder. I decided to devote some time to my book. I don't quite remember how long I was reading when the cat emitted a loud distressed meow, startled apparently by the sudden discovery of my presence. Careful not to move my head, I glanced up from my book to see her frozen in mid-stride ten feet away as she looked unwaveringly at me. She had large spooky bluish-gray eyes that unblinkingly looked directly into mine. She seemed to be trying to decide if I was a life-sized garden gnome or a living being. I returned her stare, trying as best I could not to move a muscle. This seemed to unnerve her. She emitted another loud even more menacing meow to see if I would react. I did not. This seemed to confuse her even more. Curiosity will have to kill her but one way or another she was going to find out if I was a living being. Nervously edging forward and backward and meowing every few seconds, she tentatively drew closer. Now five feet away, she raised her nostrils and sniffed the air to see if she can catch a human smell. Still, I remained motionless. Refusing to be deterred, in a rocking to-and-fro slow-motion movement, she inched her way to the foot of my chaise lounge and sniffed my moccasins.

Deciding that I had tortured her enough, I uncrossed my legs. Startled by my sudden movement, she leapt five feet into the air, emitting an ear-piercing meow. She began to meow affectionately almost the instant she landed. I called to her and invited her to come closer so that I could scratch her head. She was at my side in an instant. Ignoring the formalities of proper introductions, she hopped into my lap, purring up a blue streak.

All was well with the world. A strange Siamese cat was sitting on my lap purring to her heart's content and my avian friends continued with their melodic harmonies. It was indeed a perfect summer day.

CHAPTER 4

Caribbean Vacation

Over the years my wife Barbara and her parents told wonderful stories of their many adventures during the 1970s sailing the Adriatic, driving through Spain, shopping in the souks of Marrakech, riding the subways of Moscow, to name a few. Two of my favorites tell of the time a Moroccan prince offered her mother ten stallions, jewels, six camels and an assortment of other animals as a dowry, and of the occasions in Moscow when Barbara, sporting a serious 1960s rain-cloud afro, was repeatedly mistaken for Angela Davis, the 1960s Black Panther and political activist.

Barbara's travels no longer consist of exotic trips with her now 92-year-old wheelchair-bound dad and her 88-year-old quadruple-bypass, heart-surgery-survivor mom. She now accompanies them on a different kind of journey as they painfully navigate what Harvard psychiatrist George Vaillant calls 'the minefields of aging'.

Taking care of elderly parents takes a tremendous toll on the best of caregivers. Barbara was no exception. To do so without abandoning the commitments of her professional life was truly inspiring. She worked tirelessly to maintain a relatively high-level quality of life for her parents. When her dad lost his ability to walk, she was resolute in her efforts to assist him and became quite skilled at, among other things, transferring him from one place to another - bed to wheelchair, wheelchair to car, car to wheelchair, etc. Thanks to Barbara's superhuman efforts her parents continued to enjoy many of their lifetime pleasures and indulgences - going to concerts, museums, restaurants, socializing with friends, etc. - long after anyone would have thought possible.

Through it all, I tried to do my supportive-husband part as I continuously sought ways to help mitigate the burden Barbara so unselfishly bore. Yet, I was concerned that she was doing too much, that she needed a break from this emotionally and physically exhausting caregiving commitment. A short vacation would do her a world of good.

"How would you like to go to St. Kitts and lie on the beach for a week?" I asked, knowing that as a self-confessed beach bum she would find such an offer irresistible.

"Great idea," she said, hesitantly, adding, "Can I let you know tomorrow?"

"Sure," I said, happy she was willing to consider such a self-renewing getaway.

Two days later, grinning from ear to ear, Barbara greeted me with, "Guess what? I spoke to my parents and they would love to come with us."

I was flabbergasted. Now, I loved my in-laws dearly, but the idea of travelling with her 92-year-old wheelchair-bound dad and 88-year-old mother, four years removed from quadruple bypass heart surgery, didn't exactly make me jump for joy. The effort needed to process the logistics of such a gargantuan undertaking must have caused my brain to short-circuit because I simply stared at her, speechless, struggling to find the right response. The voice inside my head was screaming 'Are you crazy? Have you lost your mind?' What escaped my lips was a haltingly pathetic and disingenuous "Sure honey, that's a wonderful idea." Barbara, however, sensed my apprehension and the negative karma that enveloped me.

"Don't worry," she said, "everything is going to be just fine. My parents are really looking forward to seeing St. Kitts."

I was torn. I didn't want to disappoint my in-laws but I also did not see how this trip was humanly possible. Her dad could not walk and her mother's heart condition prohibits her from walking more that 50 yards before having to stop and rest. With no direct flights from NYC, traveling to St. Kitts with an octogenarian and a nonagenarian in wheelchairs would be, at the very least, a formidable challenge. Add to the mix the extra pieces of luggage necessary for transporting dietary and miscellaneous supplies, and the trip began to feel like a military deployment. I set out to demonstrate to Barbara that this was a perfect example of a bad idea camouflaged as a wonderful thought. For the next few days Barbara and I sparred over travel logistics. Each time I lunged at her with a practical problem, she parried with a specious solution, to my way of thinking anyway.

Despite my doubts, however, and with a great deal of trepidation, I eventually decided to give it a try. I would just have to fasten my seatbelt and not think of the potential bumps ahead. My anxiety notwithstanding, there was an unshakeable nagging feeling, somewhere deep in the recesses of my subconscious, that with Barbara's spirit and strength of will, we just might pull it off.

The week spent in St. Kitts was wonderful, difficult, disaster-free and filled with psychic rewards. The only real 'difficulty' came, not from the arduous nature of pushing wheelchairs and toting luggage, but from the seemingly non-stop unwanted attention we attracted. Being by nature reticent, I prefer the solitude that comes with being publicly inconspicuous.

The seemingly judgmental stares (perhaps some were stares of approval, I couldn't always tell) of the public made me uncomfortable. More than the stares, I hated the well-intentioned questions and comments which somehow left me feeling exposed. When a woman at La Guardia airport said "You will both be eternally blessed", I felt undeserving of such approbation. We were anomalies and there were those who felt compelled to make us feel that way. It was a bit much when someone suggested that Barbara and I were auditioning for sainthood.

Looking back, it is now clear to me that we accomplished such a seemingly impossible feat through the sheer force of Barbara's indomitable spirit - a spirit that enables her to see the possibilities in the face of the impossible.

My hand calluses, acquired from a week of pushing wheelchairs on a beautiful but wheelchair-unfriendly island, have long since disappeared. I now strive to challenge myself to overcome my self-perceived limitations, eternally grateful to Barbara and her parents for affording me to the opportunity to share this special journey.

CHAPTER 5

My Oldman and the Sea

I had my daily exercise bike ride in the foothills of Mt. Olivees. Tough place to ride but the hilly topography gave me a great cardio workout. Aching muscles, a good temporary elixir for what ails my aching heart.

As the family genealogist, I made a visit to the archives of the St. George's Anglican Church in Nevis, and was transported back in time. What a thrill. Somehow, entering a time capsule, warping back to the 1850s, is a lot more fun, a lot less emotionally wrenching, than sifting through dad's house. A house built with his own hands. A house filled with childhood memories inextricably mixed with the debris of his earthly life.

May 1st, eighteen hundred and fifty-seven! There it was, exquisitely written on paper yellowed with the passage of time. One hundred and fifty-five years ago, to be exact. My great grandfather's baptismal record!

Where to find solace?

The Caribbean Sea beckoned. I tried unsuccessfully to ignore its call. Tiny waves lapped gently against my ankles as I entered for a swim. At seven in the morning, there was no one about. In another half-hour this lit-tle cove with its black volcanic sand will be bathed in the direct rays of the sun, already creeping over the mountain ridge. Absorbed by the bucolic beauty and serenity of this little-used cove, I forgot, for a moment, that I was wading in the cruel waters of Bird Rock beach - the place where dad drowned suddenly, inexplicably.

Maybe it was the pristine water that sparkled in the soft, diffused light of the early morning sun; maybe it was the hypnotic, rhythmic murmur-ings of the tiny waves breaking gently on shore. Maybe, just maybe, the soothing calm that enveloped me as I swam - a pain-mitigating calm - was Poseidon's special gift to me. A peace-offering from the very same waters that literally washed away dad's last breath.

Drawn by some unseen force, I returned, again and again, to be con-soled, to be held closely in the warm embrace of this murderous, life-giving and restorative sea.

CHAPTER 6

Peter's Performance

I was sitting in my office diligently figuring out the next day's proctoring schedule when the sound of voices raised in anger reached my ears. The din was coming from two doors down the corridor. As I approached the source of the disturbance I was able to immediately identify the sound of Peter's unmistakable voice. It was unmistakable not because of any special tonal quality or pitch, but more because of its style. Sure enough, when I got to the classroom, there was Peter, holding court. I paused for a while in the threshold of the doorway and took in the performance. And what a performance it was! He was the only student standing, an overturned desk lying at his feet. His classmates were seated quietly; their eyes focused on him. I tried to interpret what I saw in the silent faces of his absorbed audience. The teacher stood with her back to the chalkboard, chalk in hand, looking on with an air of helpless resignation mixed with disgust. There was a sense that she had seen Peter's act before, except that this time it had a more intense and theatrical quality. It was truly a tour de force. The look on the faces of his classmates seemed to suggest either ennui from seeing (yet again) a tired and worn-out act, or curiosity about the mental stability of the speaker.

The target of Peter's attack was a female classmate who supposedly had stepped on his notebook when it fell to the floor. The diatribe went on for about two minutes - a monologue pregnant with every possible curse word imaginable. The fact that the Assistant Principal was standing at the door, arms folded across his chest as he observed the whole scene did not seem to faze him one bit. The curse words and filth fell from his lips with shocking fluidity and ease. His monologue included all of the standards – mother****er, b**ch, ho, a****le and others not familiar to my uncultured ears.

I asked Peter to leave the classroom and report to my office. I braced myself. As he walked past me, he unleashed a new volley of obscenities for good measure.

Peter is an otherwise normal fourteen-year-old eighth grader who happens to have a special propensity for using foul language. He is a pro who has honed this skill to perfection. Hands down, he is the best fourteen-year-old foul-mouthed student I have ever met. Interestingly, Peter is not a violent kid. He is a rotund chubby-faced kid with a charming smile whose overall demeanor belies his filthy mouth. He never gets into verbal or physical fights with boys - he knows that they can all kick his butt, and prefers the company of girls, especially those dyed-in-the-wool, card-carrying members of the he-say-she-say club. Very often when there is a conflict between eighth grade girls, twice per day occurrences, on average, Peter's name can be found smack dab in the middle.

Earlier in the school year I called Peter's mother to talk to her about his foul mouth. As soon as I identified myself she greeted me with, "What the f**k did he do now?" I must admit that in all my years in education and countless phone calls to parents, this was a first-time experience. I was startled by the sudden and violent nature of the words. I calmly pointed out that I do not speak in that manner and would therefore appreciate it if she did not curse. She quickly explained that although she used the word f**k, she was clearly not cursing at me. This was indeed a very important distinction to her. To her credit, later in the conversation she felt compelled to apologize (or at least to soften the harshness of her words) by saying:

"You know Mr. Simmonds, you need to understand that this is the way that we speak in the hood."

Peter uses the same logic whenever I admonish him for his gratuitous cursing. After my telephone conversation with his mother, it became quite clear that rehabilitating Peter would not be an easy task.

I gave Peter a letter to take home and made certain that he understood that when he returned to school he must be accompanied by a responsible adult. He suggested to me that his sister would be the one coming to confer with me. The last adult who came to school on Peter's behalf was indeed one of his sisters, a woman of about twenty-five. I remembered that she handled Peter well and said all the right things. I secretly hoped that she would return again.

The next day, Friday, as the students came streaming into the entrance, I saw Peter coming down the hallway towards me. He was alone.

"Is someone here with you?" I asked. "No, my sister is away and cannot be here before Monday," he replied. "In that case," I said, "you will have to go back home immediately and return with an adult. I thought I made it abundantly clear that you are not to return alone."

We went to the main office to telephone his sister. I learned earlier that Peter has five sisters, all above the age of twenty-five. There was no answer.

"You will have to remain seated in the office until the secretary can reach someone from your home." I left the office, ignoring his protestations.

Two hours later the secretary informed me that Peter's sister was on the phone. Apparently, Peter had left the school without permission and went to his sister's house to tell her his sob story. I picked up the phone and before I could say one word, a volley of obscenities came blasting from the earpiece of the telephone. According to her, I had done her brother wrong by throwing him out on the street and not permitting him to contact a family member by phone. Every attempt I made to describe what actually occurred was summarily cut short with a new barrage of obscenities. Just before I decided to hang up the phone, she cut loose with a barrage of expletives. It was remarkable. I counted eight consecutive f**k you issued in rapid succession before I lowered the phone into its cradle. I immediately had misgivings about hanging up on her. It would have been interesting to hear the full gamut of her profanity. This must be one of the other sisters whom I had not met. The sister I met was relatively sophisticated. This could not be her, I thought. At least I hoped not.

Two days went by before the secretary called to inform me that Peter and his sister were waiting to see me in the main office. It was a State testing day and I had neither the time nor the inclination to entertain Peter and his family. I could feel my heartbeat quicken. Which sister was this? I was certainly not in the mood for anymore gratuitous cursing. This violent use of language always has a tremendous effect on me. It leaves me totally exhausted physically and emotionally. I was so swamped with post-test administrative tasks that I soon forgot that they were waiting. Test materials were due at the district office in an hour.

Forty-five minutes later I was still knee deep in paperwork when Peter and his sister, tired of waiting to see me, walked into my office. It was the sister I had met, the non-abrasive relatively sophisticated one. Thank heavens. She couldn't be the one who was so nasty on the phone, could she? I was no longer certain. I invited them both to sit. I told her the story of what transpired, starting from the day Peter staged that grand performance for his classmates. Her demonstration of patience and poise as she listened made me feel that this was going to be a productive conference. I had the right sister. I was now certain of it. When I described my earlier telephone conversations with one of their other (foul-mouthed) sister, she smiled and said, "Now you know why Peter has such a filthy mouth. You don't know how many times my mother has attempted to wash his mouth out with soap."

She then began to explain to Peter in my presence, just like she did the last time she came to school for a conference, the importance of showing respect to teachers and peers. She turned to me and explained that she was making Peter her personal project because she realized that he needed a steady hand to guide him. Until now, she said, nobody in the family had given him the guidance he needed.

I wrapped up the conference by assuring her that I will continue to work with Peter until he graduated in June, assuring her that I would not give up on him. She responded that, likewise, she would be always there for her little brother. I also thanked her for being so positive and for her support. She had asked me earlier for a copy of Peter's behavioral anecdotes that I kept on my computer. I printed them and handed them to her. She sat for a moment reading the sheet. I examined her face closely for clues to her reaction to her brother's episodic outbursts. Her face told me nothing. After reading the text she folded the paper, placed it in her bag, turned to face Peter and said:

"What the f**k is wrong with you? Don't let me ever hear again that you f***king talk to teachers that way."

CHAPTER 7

Tower Flight 222

10:35 AM

The lines at the check-in counter at LAX were unusually long as travelers gave themselves extra time in anticipation of the usual knee-jerk reaction of the airlines which, for about a year after a major airplane crash, tend to increased check-in-security ten-fold. As I scanned the faces of my fellow travelers, I saw images of travelers who came to the airport equipped with an extra suitcase-load of patience. A sort of nervous anxiety pervaded the atmosphere. It was less than a week since TWA flight 800 crashed into the Atlantic Ocean twelve minutes after taking off from JFK. At the very least, the public's confidence in air travel was shaken.

12:00 PM

I sat near gate 12 awaiting the departure of my 12:45 PM flight back to JFK, and tried my very best to occupy my thoughts so as not to think of what could go wrong. As I pored over my crossword puzzle an elderly woman approached and sat next to me. I looked up and acknowledged her.

"I guess it's back to New York," she said, trying to break the ice.

There was an eccentric quality about her. It was enough to make me think, 'Oh no! I hope she does not bend my ear for the next half-hour before we board.' Perhaps it was her getup. She was a woman of about 75, dressed like a 30 something. If she was much younger (I find it impossible to be impolite to the elderly) I could be downright rude, and she would be certain not to bother me. Without being discourteous I gave a perfunctory reply and immediately buried my head in my crossword puzzle. I hoped she could read body language because this body was saying that it does not want to be bothered. After about two minutes she tried to engage the other person sitting next to her. She received the same cold-shoulder treatment.

12:30 PM

I was pondering the answer to 5 Down when a voice crackled over the public announcement system informing us that it was time to board. I gathered my knapsack and thought to myself, 'Heaven help the passengers unlucky to be assigned seats next to my elderly eccentric.' I boarded the plane and headed down the aisle to seat 17G. I was relieved to see that there were no seats immediately in front of row G.

'Good,' I thought, grateful for the extra leg room.

Finding room for long legs is always a problem for those of us who habitually travel in coach. I settled into my seat, reached for my seat belt and looked across the aisle to my right. There she was in 17A! My elderly eccentric. She was fumbling to connect the seat belt across her ample midriff. I breathed a sigh of relief. It could be worse, after all. She could be sitting next to me.

12:40 PM

"Excuse me ma'am, I think you are in my seat."

My heart skipped a beat at the sound of these words. I looked up from my puzzle and saw a gentleman addressing 17A!

"Oh, I'm sorry," said my elderly eccentric, and began searching in her purse for her boarding pass. She found it and handed it to the gentleman who was trying to displace her. She seemed annoyed that she would have to move.

"You are in 17F," he announced.

Oh no! I thought, The Fates have conspired against me. I promptly began to look around the cabin for empty seats. I didn't see any at first glance. Maybe I'll pretend I'm going to the bathroom, locate an empty seat and never return to 17G. There was no way I was going to submit myself to meaningless chatter for 5 hours. I was still stunned and pondering my fate when she cheerfully greeted me.

"Oh nice, we have seats together," she chirped gleefully.

It was too late. I should have left before she had a chance to notice me. I was trapped.

12:50 PM

"Ladies and gentlemen, sorry for the delay. We are having some problems closing the cargo hold. We expect to have it fixed in the next few minutes, then we'll be on our way."

There did not seem to be anything unusual about the captain's announcement. I continued working on my puzzle, hoping that my body still spoke a clear coherent language. A language which said, "Do not disturb!"

1:30 PM

"Ladies and gentlemen, we haven't had any success getting the cargo hold secured. We will have to take the plane to be serviced. I'm afraid we have to ask everyone to deplane. We are very sorry for this inconvenience. When you deplane, please report to the ticket counter where you will receive a $15 lunch voucher. You should report back to gate 12 at 5:00 PM to find out the new boarding time."

I was surprised at how calmly everyone received this news. It was clear from the buzz that everyone was disappointed though far from being outraged. It meant that our departure would be delayed at least 5 hours. As I left the plane it occurred to me that there must be more to the captain's story than met the eye. There must be a security problem that Tower did not want to divulge for fear of alarming the passengers. They were probably going to use the next few hours to make a clean sweep of the plane. Maybe I should return to NY on another airline. Then again, flight 222 will probably be the safest flight by the time they are done thoroughly checking the plane. I decided to go get my lunch, find a quiet corner and read until it was time to board.

4:45 PM

As I walked back to the gate I wondered what happened to 17F. I was quite certain there would be lots of available empty seats because when we deplaned I overheard several passengers saying that they would try to find another carrier back to New York. At 5 o'clock there was an announcement indicating that we may board for the new departure time of 5:30 PM.

5:15 PM

As we settled into our seats I began to plot my seat-changing strategy. I would make my move after the captain removed the *Fasten Your Seat belts* sign. Suddenly 17F interrupted my thoughts.

"Would you like a banana?" she asked.

Boy, is she clever! She offers me a banana so that I might feel obliged to be her captive audience for 5 transcontinental hours.

6:00 PM

"Ladies and gentlemen, again we apologize for the delay. A gentleman just came forward and asked to deplane, which means that we have to locate his luggage in the cargo hold. As you know, it is our policy not to take passengers unaccompanied by their luggage. We should be leaving in another half hour."

For the first time I detected a murmur of protest from these otherwise extremely patient passengers. The captain, the delay and the whole situation were finally plumbing the depths of their patience.

"This is getting ridiculous!" said a voice a few rows behind me.

6:10 PM

17F explained to me that she had a hearing problem and asked if I could recount the captain's announcements. What a clever ruse, my eccentric friend. You really are determined to engage me in conversation, aren't you? Until this moment, I had avoided all eye contact and sent nonstop non-verbal cues to indicate my desire to be left alone. Her desire to unburden her soul was so palpable I could feel her furtive glances bouncing off the side of my face as she looked for an opening. Unfortunately, she took my explanation of the captain's words as a signal of my willingness to chat. Before I knew what hit me, she began talking. Dispensing with the normal introductory formalities of strangers meeting for the first time, I immediately became, to my surprise, an old family friend. Perhaps this would be a good time to employ my favorite travel-stress coping mechanism. It has always been an interesting exercise when I'm running late and I'm totally at the mercy of bus, trains and planes, to 'remove' myself from the situation by observing how others deal with their stress. Maybe I should just surrender and listen to my elderly eccentric. Listening to her might be interesting. It did not seem to matter to her that I was totally ignorant of who Betsy and Maggie were. As she kept mentioning names of people who I suspected were family members, I thought of interrupting her to ask her to explain the references. I decided not to. What the heck, it was a 5-hour flight. It will all become clear eventually. Or will it? Twenty minutes into her monologue I suddenly realized that she was not the type who required any occasional listener-verification comments like:

"I see."

"Oh, really?"

"No kidding!"

"You don't say!"

She was now totally absorbed in her story. And me with her, even though most of what she said made sense only to her. Her story was freely articulated, though disjointed and haphazard in its sequences, akin to that of a child telling a story.

6:15 PM

"My son flies glider planes......... we went to Las Vegas last weekend. It was fun. Have you been to Las Vegas recently? When my husband was alive we stayed at the Mirage. They have rides there and everything. My son says they have rides on top of the building! Have you ever been to Atlantic City? No? You're kidding! At 13, my granddaughter was playing the crap tables. She was tall for her age then."

"Ira, you should write this stuff down. Looks like it's going to be an interesting story," I said to myself. I took out my yellow pad and started writing as she rambled on. What would I tell her if she asked me what I was writing? I'll have to make up a story, I guess. She didn't seem to notice, or care, that I was writing as she was telling me her story.

"We went to Morrow beach. *I* had to rent a van. You don't know the half of it!...my daughter-in-law thinks she is the Madonna of Scientology. Do you know what that is? You know, with L. Ron Hubbard?" She paused for a few seconds before continuing.

"How could anybody make me hear better if what I really need is an operation?" Another pause as she looked around as if trying to find a flight attendant.

"Looks like we'll never leave, huh? My friend says, why don't you fly Tower? You'll save at least a hundred dollars." She leaned forward, reached under the seat for her purse, opened it, rummaged around until she found her mirror, crookedly applied some lipstick and attempted to straighten her wig.

"My son, he has problems, …if you know what I mean."

I didn't know what she meant. 'Why don't you tell me what you mean?' I thought.

For the first time she seemed to notice that I was writing. She paused for a few seconds and asked.

"What are you writing?"

Oh oh, here it comes. I had been furiously recording her words for at least 40 minutes.

"I'm making a list of things I need to do for my upcoming trip to New Hampshire." I lied.

"I hear there is a Coney Island up there, with rides and everything."

I was bewildered by her response. I had no idea what she was talking about but my fear that she might ask follow-up questions about my New Hampshire trip disappeared as she promptly continued her story.

6:30 PM

"Don't you think this is awful?" She was referring to the fact that we still had not departed LAX. "For another hundred bucks I could have flown American……. I didn't know they had classes in Tower!…….My son is a drug addict. He is the biggest disappointment in my life - besides my other son not continuing with his music… Someone told me I should get one of those car phones. What do you call them?"

"Cellular phones." I said.

"You mean you can call from anywhere? ...... She would ask a question but would not wait for a response. "I'm a widow, you know. Since my husband died I've been all alone. I'm not accustomed to traveling by myself. We did *everything* together, you know."

6:40 PM

The captain's voice once again penetrated the cabin.

"Another passenger has asked to deplane and each time this occurs we have to locate his bags and this takes about 45 minutes. Sorry for the delay".

A passenger in the back of the plane totally lost it after hearing this latest announcement.

"Tell me who it is and I'll kick his ass," he screamed at the top of his lungs.

"Where's my hat. Oh my, it looks like someone took my hat. Stewardess!" said 17F realizing that she had misplaced her hat. "It is so hard since my husband died," she continued. "We used to do *everything* together. He didn't really like to travel. We used to go to all the shows."

Once again, the captain announced:

"Ladies and gentlemen, a few passengers have convinced the last passenger not to deplane. I would like to thank these gentlemen for their assistance."

A great cheer and a thunderous applause resounded throughout the cabin.

"Yeah!" screamed a woman immediately behind me.

Airborne

6:50 PM (PST) to 3:30 AM (EST)

Tower Flight 222 slowly taxied from the gate to queue up for take-off.

"He was such a good musician. I can't understand why he gave it up. He was so talented. It just breaks my heart. I went to hear him play once and when a woman found out he was my son she asked me how come I produced such a talented musician." There was a 10 second pause before she continued.

"I don't really like to talk about it. He's a drug addict." She had switched to her other son. "That's what he is. A brilliant guy, but a drug addict. It's so sad. He supports his habit playing the stock market. It's so sad. He's no good. He still lives with me. I can't seem to get rid of him. I really don't like to talk about it, but he is just no good."

She got up and headed in the direction of the bathroom. I wrote frantically as I tried to fill in the gaps before she came back to her seat. She returned 10 minutes later.

"I just took a Tylenol. My friend is supposed to meet me. She'll be calling the airport, right? To find out what time I get in? I bought extra insurance for this trip and I never do that... I tell you, I can do without Mexican food for the rest of my life. I don't care for Mexican food." What reminded her of Mexican food at this precise moment was unclear to me.

There was silence for the next two minutes. I glanced at her and noticed that she was asleep. I took the opportunity to look at her more closely. Was she Jewish or Italian? I couldn't tell. One moment she seemed to be one, another moment she seemed to be the other. She did look somewhat Italian yet there was a Jewish quality about her. What exactly? I couldn't tell. She did not sound Jewish but yet she spoke in a Jewish manner. On her right hand she wore 2 gaudy-looking rings with extremely large fake stones. She wore black leggings which were much too tight. Black blouse, lacy and low-cut. Over it a denim jacket with silver studs. I got the feeling she was trying to look expensively elegant but she managed instead to look like a cheap hooker. Her nails were painted bright red. On her head was a bleach blond wig.

"Since my husband died two years ago, (she was now awake and talking) it has been so hard to find people who would go out with me. My husband was always good to them but they all dropped me when he died. I try to invite people out but they are always too busy. My son says I'm buying their friendship. They don't invite me anywhere. I know I don't look too young right now, I'm over 70 you know, but when I dress up, you know, with makeup, nice black dress, stockings, I look much younger...... I don't understand, nobody wants to go out with me........My doctor is gay..... I just love Manhattan....... He lives in Manhattan. He is *so* nice to me. I feel like I'm visiting a friend when I go to see him. He is *really* nice. When I go to shows in Manhattan, he says, why don't you stay over? It's such a long haul to Mill Basin."

Mill Basin. Where was Mill Basin? My mind was now racing. Isn't that one of those Italian strongholds, deep in the bowels of Brooklyn? Aha! I got it! She must be Italian. She continued to ramble on.

"He always has lots of food. I eat *so* much when I'm there." The thought of food must have reminded her that she still had some bananas.

"I have an extra banana, you're sure you don't want one?"

I told her I was sure. She quickly resumed her saga.

"Doctors make a lot of money but he does not charge me much. He's so nice to me. His roommate used to take care of an elderly woman who died and left him all her money. Seven hundred thousand dollars! Can you imagine that?"

She dozed off again. Meals were being served when she awoke.

"Oh, are we getting some goodies?" she yawned, rubbing her hands in glee. When her meal came she ate with her fingers.

"Stewardess, I need a knife to cut my chicken."

She did not wait for the knife, using instead her spoon and fork.

"Would you like my cake?" I said no thanks.

"Are you sure? The coffee was rather good. Do you like coffee? Since I'm alone so much now, I've been using instant coffee. I put cinnamon in my coffee."

Never mind the coffee, I thought. Let's get back to the doctor's roommate. That's much more interesting. The disjointed and random way in which her thoughts fell from her lips meant that there was no guarantee she would return to the topic. I would just have to prompt her.

"What does the doctor's roommate do for a living?" I asked, breaking my silent vow not to interrupt her.

"Do for a living?" she repeated with a loud laugh. She was surprised and amused by the question.

"He's an alcoholic," she replied.

"Isn't that something? All he does is get drunk. What a life!" She threw her head back and laughed again as she said this, as though remembering some private hilarious episode of his insobriety.

"Isn't that something? God forgive me for saying this, but thank God they don't have any kids." It took a few seconds to realize that she was now referring to her daughter-in-law. "She's too fat! Much too fat. I'm not kidding. She's a girl with a pretty face and all, but boy, is she fat! I can't tell you! She's a real yenta. You know what that is?" She seemed eager to steep me in Yiddish lore. Maybe she was Jewish, after all. Or both. I pretended not to know what a yenta was.

"A fish woman," she said. I wanted to ask her to elaborate but as she was on a roll I decided not to distract her.

"They don't cook. They eat out all the time……. And guess *who* pays every time? Me. My girl friend tells me that I could have gone to Europe on the money I spend on my son and his wife. Next time I go back there I'll just play dumb." A few seconds went by before she added,

"And broke……..since my husband died everything has changed. When you get old everything bothers you. When I was young I wouldn't bother. Now I worry about every little thing. I'm betwixt and between, that's why I'm so aggravated. Don't know why I'm telling you this, a complete stranger. Why am I telling you my life story? Maybe I should talk to a priest. Do you think that would help?"

I told her I thought it would.

"He's brilliant, my son. He always gets 90s." She seemed genuinely grieved by her son's drug problem.

"He received a scholarship to study radiology at Downstate. What does he do? He falls asleep in his classes. It's the drugs… I guess drugs don't go well with radiology," she added with a note of helpless resignation, extremely worried that no one would be at JFK to meet her. There had been so many delays that we were now scheduled to land at 3:30 am.

"You should see the junk my daughter-in-law packed in my suitcase for her mother. How am I going to lift that suitcase? I should not have accepted all that stuff."

3:40 AM EST

We are finally at JFK. When we got to the baggage pickup area she could not find one of her bags. She was completely undone. Finding only one claim ticket attached to her ticket jacket, I asked if she was certain that she checked two bags. She assured me she had, and began whimpering like a helpless child.

"Oh, what am I going to do? Oh, ohhhh, what am I going to do?"

There was a bit of a quiver in her voice, as she seemed on the verge of tears.

"Don't worry," I said, scanning the conveyor belt for signs of the lost bag she had just described, "it is probably on its way out."

But even as I tried to reassure her, I wondered if she did indeed check two bags. She looked up at me with her big blue eyes, crookedly marked with black eyeliner which by now, at 3:50 in the morning, was so smudged that it gave her the appearance of a badly made-up drag queen. She repeated the same doleful refrain.

"Oh, ohhhh, what am I going to do? My whole life is in that bag."

On the brink of tears, she looked at me pleadingly. Her whole life was in a bag that was probably lost! No wonder she was so upset. An elderly friendless widow about to confront the daunting task of reconstructing her life. The thought of having to replace all of her important papers and credit cards must at that moment seem overwhelming and impossible. But why didn't she keep these valuable items on her person? She no longer seemed eccentric, just wretched. My heart went out to her. Her blue eyes were now swimming in the clear liquid of her tears. She seemed as vulnerable as a newborn puppy.

"You have to do something about my predicament," she pleaded.

I wanted to help but I did not know what to do. After all, I am just a stranger who happened to be sitting next to her on a bi-coastal flight. But by now I was no stranger. She undoubtedly ceased to regard me as such the moment I began to show interest in her story. That very moment signaled my initiation into her tiny fraternity of friends. Her "friends" have probably deserted her because of their unwillingness to listen to her endless saga of loneliness and depression.

I was moved by her sadness and her growing state of panic. She continued to demand that I do something.

"What exactly do you have in the bag?" I asked. Perhaps, I thought, I can relieve some of her anxiety by assuring her that the documents in her bag can be easily replaced. She would certainly need to call her credit card companies to inform them of her loss.

"Oh, ohhhh, what am I going to do? My whole life is in that bag."

I must get her to tell me the names of her credit card companies so that we can notify them immediately.

"What's in the bag?" I asked again.

"My pills and my makeup," she replied.

CHAPTER 8

West Indian Hot Sauce

A irline check-in at the St. Kitts Airport for my return flight back home to NYC. My checked bag was 2 lbs. over the allowable limit. My options were (1) pay a US$100 fee or (2) transfer 2 lbs. from my checked bag to my carry-on.

I chose option 2.

As I went through security the agent stopped the conveyor belt, removed my carry-on and instructed a colleague to search it.

The agent started to unzip my bag but was called away to inspect the carry-on bag belonging to the traveler next in line. When he was done he returned to my carry-on. Before he could resume searching my bag he was called away once again to inspect the carry-on of yet another traveler **behind** me. He never returned. A female agent came in his stead and resumed searching my bag. After a few seconds she asked me to give her a sec, she'll be right back. I responded with:

"Sorry, I've given enough secs to both you and your colleague. You may not assist any more travelers in line **behind** me. First you will finish inspecting my bag, **then** you may go elsewhere." She started to protest, thought better of it and dug into my carry-on, probing in search of the item flagged by the scanner.

"Sir, I will have to confiscate this. It contains more than three ounces."

In the agent's plastic-gloved right hand was a bottle of West Indian hot sauce. I had removed it earlier from my checked bag to lighten its weight. I heard myself say, "Not a problem, I understand," words that belied my anger at the confiscation of my precious hot sauce. Finished with her search, she waved me on. I zipped up my carry-on and watched in horror as she dropped the beautiful reddish-brown bottle of hot sauce, concocted by some faceless Kittitian woman for the prandial delight of spicy-food lovers, into a garbage bin labeled 'Confiscated'.

Then, inexplicably, as the agent turned to assist the next traveler, my right arm (having a mind of its own) led me to the garbage bin, pushed down the swivel lid, located the hot sauce and removed it from the bin. As my arm withdrew itself from the bin it inadvertently knocked off the lid which fell to the floor with a thud. As calmly as I could, with heart racing a mile a minute, I picked it up, placed it atop the bin and proceeded on to the waiting area.

I don't know why the female agent did not stop me. Standing only a few feet away she had to have heard the lid fall. As I sat in the waiting area I expected at any moment to hear the PA system spring to life with:

"*The West Indian hot sauce gentleman, please report to Counter A*".

"*Will the gentleman who retrieve the hot sauce from the garbage please identify yourself*".

"It has been reported that a bottle of West Indian hot sauce is missing from the 'Confiscated' bin. Flight 1444 will not depart until said hot sauce is returned."

The anticipated announcement concerning the hot sauce which I stole from myself never came. I breathed a sigh of relief only **after** my plane was airborne.

Miami airport. Feeling rather smug, having thwarted the attempt to separate me from my West Indian hot sauce, I marched to the baggage claim to collect my checked luggage. I was quite tickled (and truly surprised) at my unprecedented act of derring-do. Still silently singing my praises, I cleared customs and turned my checked luggage over to American Airlines. A few minutes later I was whistling my way to the security clearance line.

Then, like a sudden attack of agita, I was hit with a sickening feeling of despair. My precious West Indian hot sauce was still in my carry-on. In my giddiness over its triumphant rescue at the St. Kitts airport I had forgotten to transfer it to my checked luggage.

The patron goddess of West Indian hot sauce, will she intervene once more? It took the security agent all of twenty seconds to locate the 'explosive' hot sauce. A world record, I dare say, for the number of times the same bottle of hot sauce was confiscated by two different agents, in two different time zones, in two different countries.

She did not recklessly toss it into the garbage. She held it lovingly, admiringly in both hands in a show of empathy for my loss - as though she understood my pain, as if to reassure me that my West Indian hot sauce was going to a better place. However, I couldn't shake that uneasy feeling that as soon as I'm out of sight my West Indian hot sauce will be lying at the bottom of a garbage can.

"It will be kept it in that secure room over there," she said with a smile.

CHAPTER 9

The Man

It was a balmy summer day in July on Lake Chautauqua, a few miles from my sister's home in Northwest New York. I tried to maneuver the sunfish so that the sail would catch the gentle breeze that wafted across the lake. It was not the best day for sailing. Jackie, my fifteen-year-old niece, was sitting next to me in excited anticipation. This was her first sailing experience and I wanted it to be just as exhilarating as the first time my wife took me out on a lake in the White Mountains of New Hampshire. Just a mere hint of a wake was visible as the sunfish inched its way through the glossy surface. This was the first time Jackie had been on a sunfish sailboat and from the look on her face I could tell she was ready for an adventure.

Jackie let out a gleeful scream as the wind suddenly picked up. I quickly came about and adjusted the sheet. With the sail pregnant with the long-awaited wind, the sunfish lurched forward and we were off.

Looking back in the distance, I could see Mother standing on the dock. She seemed disoriented as she looked about her in the manner of someone who was lost. Louisa, my nine-year-old niece, and Jr., my seventeen-year-old nephew, appeared to be trying to console her. We came about and headed back to the dock. I was concerned that Mother might be getting too agitated. When we docked Louisa explained that Mother was asking for the whereabouts of *the man.*

It had been about a year and a half since Mother, then 73 years old, was diagnosed as having Alzheimer's. I was still trying to come to grips with the fact that this debilitating disease had afflicted her. It afflicts about six million people in the U.S. and, so far, no cure has been found. Some of the symptoms include severe memory loss, paranoia, severe depression and sudden states of agitation. The loss of an Alzheimer patient's intellectual abilities is such that it severely disrupts normal social and occupational function.

To be referred to by Mother as *the man* evoked bittersweet feelings of both alienation and endearment. On one hand it meant that she did not know who I was. Earlier in the year, my brother called me and told me that Mother did not remember that she had two sons. It was inconceivable to me that this could happen. That was the first time I felt overwhelmed by a real sense of loss. I remember thinking at the time, "Is it possible that Mother could suddenly forget that she gave birth to two sons?"

On the other hand, it reminded me of a time thirty years earlier. My parents were separated and, as the eldest son, Mother anointed me *the man* of the house. This was a rite of passage for me and a time when I learned a great deal from Mother. The most powerful images and impressions that remain with me even today are those of a proud and stoic woman who provided for and nurtured us the only way she knew how: with dogged determination, serene dignity and a fierce sense of independence.

This summer was the first time I had the opportunity to take care of her since the onset of Alzheimer's. The weeks spent with Mother gave me some invaluable insights that enabled me to understand, somewhat, the physical and emotional effects of Alzheimer's on her and on our family. Before now, the full impact of the illness was totally lost on me. I was suddenly hit with the sobering realization that I would never again be able to hold a normal conversation with Mother. Other family members had related frightful incidents. There was the time when she got out of my brother's car, crossed the street in traffic and approached a nearby policeman to inform him that she was being kidnapped. On other occasions she would pack a suitcase and announce determinedly that she was going *home.*

Although I understood the medical evidence which suggests that there are organic factors etiologically related to changes within her brain, at first, I still tried to make sense of her pronouncements by trying to reason with her. This was usually an exercise in futility. She frequently forgets words or uses them incorrectly. I quickly learned the technique of abruptly changing the subject or distracting her before she became too frustrated at not being able to make herself understood. I continually tried to seek ways to make her feel that she was not incoherent. By so doing, I think I achieved some measure of success at mitigating her tension, frustration, embarrassment and anger.

There were wonderful moments when her great sense of humor surfaced, but especially joyful were those rare fleeting times when I was certain she recognized me. To date, the only noticeable evidence of positive identification occurs when Mother asks about Sophie, my eleven-year-old daughter. Sophie now represents (and will always represent) a spiritual connection between Mother and me.

Mother is the wisest person I've ever known. It was always a source of wonder to me that she could be so wise. Even at the stage of my life when I knew it all (as a teenager), there was something about the way (it was imbued with quiet eloquence) in which she disseminated her wisdom that always gave me pause. Inexplicably, through some intuitive predisposition, I always knew that she was right. I never told her (or anyone for that matter) how much I secretly trusted her judgement, even though I might have acted to the contrary. I now wish I had the courage or the maturity (or whatever it took) to tell her, before her onset of Alzheimer's. But then again, maybe she already knew. There was very little that escaped her. I did not realize it at the time, but I now know that I learned most of life's important lessons from Mother. Everything I've learned from her (from social values to the social graces) has served me well in my life-long journey in search of self-fulfillment. For this I'm eternally grateful.

It feels strange to speak of Mother in the past tense. Although she is still physically with us, the progress of the disease is such that she is only a frail image of her former self. In coming to grips with this loss, I find it far more therapeutic to think of the innumerable positive aspects of her life. I suspect that Mother would not want us to think of her in her present memory-deprived condition, but rather, in her previous state, before her short-term memory-loss drastically changed her personality.

I recently discovered a photograph of Mother, taken when she was in her late twenties. I showed it to her and asked if she knew who it was. Her response was as revealing as it was reassuring. She promptly responded that it was a woman by the name of Sarah (Mother's name). Referring to her pre-Alzheimer self in the third person as she did, seems to be one of the mechanisms Mother now uses to deal with this devastating loss of control. Always a demure, dignified and independent woman, she now has to depend on others (strangers, as far as she is concerned) to assist her with the simplest tasks. It is indeed comforting to know that she is finding ways to cope with the effects of the disease. This type of resourcefulness has always characterized Mother's will to overcome all odds.

Each day, as I try to guide, inspire and motivate my charges (twelve and thirteen-year-old students who struggle daily to beat perhaps even greater odds), I can only hope that in some small way I imparted to them some of the legacy of my mother's endowment.

CHAPTER 10

New School Year

B urnout is a word frequently used in the lexicon of urban high school educators. Teachers, when describing the trajectory of their professional life frequently refer to their era of idealism, that time of their professional lives when psychic rewards abound, that time when they declare that 'I'm going to make a difference in the world by transforming the lives of kids'. If you are lucky, or rather, if you enter the profession with a purity of heart, a spirit totally devoid of selfish motives, a deep-felt conviction that every child can learn, a willingness to be reflective about your work, you may be fortunate to keep at bay the career crippling feelings of helplessness and frustration of no longer being able to 'reach' students. One of the keys to surviving the difficult daily challenges and stress of teaching, motivating, guiding, supporting inner-city teenagers, that is to say, to maintaining one's sanity and sense of purpose, is to know how to take proper care of oneself.

And so, there I was properly taking care of myself, recharging my emotional and spiritual battery as it were, enjoying the last few days of my annual August sojourn on Martha's Vineyard, when the path of my twenty-three-year tenure at the New York City Department of Education took a surprisingly bizarre twist. Bizarre, even by New York City Department of Education standards.

Just a few days remained before administrators were due back for the start of the new school year, and my annual late-summer recurring nightmares were already causing a noticeable rise in anxiety. Usually, at the end of every summer I come to expect, like the unwelcomed yet unavoidable arrival of a Fall cold, the onslaught of these nightmares. Not the kind of terror-filled blood and gore nightmares where death, my death, is imminent - the kind where the monster is in relentless pursuit with the single-minded purpose of doing terrible things to me - making me its pre-lunch snack, for example - and it is gaining rapidly, despite its slow-as-a-tortoise pace and my faster-than-a-bullet speed. No, not that deadly, bloody, flesh-tearing carnage of a nightmare, but deadly nonetheless, in a gentler and kinder sort of way. Deadly in the bloodless unfunny way a standup comic dies on stage.

Actually, referring to them as 'recurring nightmares' is not quite accurate. These were actually not the same late August dreams that haunt me each year. Rather, they are a set of dreams, different in content from year to year but all seemingly tied together by a common thread. A variation on a theme, if you will. The theme: It is the first day of school, I'm super subject-matter-prepared, my charges sit patiently, optimistically wide-eyed, endowed with promise and excited about the eternal possibilities of a new school year. They sit, waiting to be inspired, motivated, and challenged. I'm at my articulate best as I address my charges, but the vocal folds within my larynx and other physiological apparatus responsible for producing sounds refuse to function. I am speaking but my words cannot not be heard and I begin to die a slow death. How ironic was it that words, in this case the lack thereof, the ability to effectively communicate with students (a teacher's stock-in-trade), now became the instruments of my death?

So here I am, preparing myself psychologically for the start of the new school year. In the middle of August, I checked my e-mail and saw that there was a message from my principal. It said that one of our English teachers, Mr. James, left the school to take a teaching position elsewhere. Trying to replace faculty members in August is the bane of every school administrator's existence. Starting the school year with vacancies makes it almost impossible to set that all-important right tone. You know the tone. The one that sends an unambiguous message to students and parents saying that we are serious about the education of our charges. This message loses serious traction, this tone is dangerously compromised, if on the first day of school students are greeted with chaos. Very difficult to hit the ground running, to give the semblance of preparedness and order with less than a full complement of faculty and staff. I must call the principal to discuss strategy for replacing Mr. James. With no reception on my cell at this remote part of the island, I jumped on my bike and headed to receptivity.

The phone rang, the principal answered. We chatted briefly about Mr. James' departure and a strategy for replacing him. She then wanted to know if I had heard the news. What news? I asked. She politely refused to tell, without saying she won't tell. Eventually, she instructed me to find a computer and Google her name, a suggestion replete with a tis-better-if-you-discover-the-surprise-for-yourself tone. I'm always open to pleasant surprises. It would be much more interesting, not to mention rewarding, if I 'accidentally stumbled' upon this surprise.

As an educator, it is powerfully rewarding when you see your students use their imagination and ability to reason, subsequently experiencing the magic of discovery as they stumble upon the switch that turns on their individual light bulbs. And isn't it much more enjoyable as a child to discover a dollar under one's pillow as opposed to having your mother say, here's a dollar? Perhaps the principal had won an award. Maybe she was being recognized in some special way.

I mounted my bike and headed back to the house, pondering as I pedaled what exciting news awaits me at the end of my cyber search. Not that I was at all surprised by her reluctance to divulge the nature of this news. To date we had worked together for just a year as administrators (she as Principal and I as an Assistant Principal) of this relatively small 200 student alternative high school. It was clear from the beginning that I was not hired as a collaborative administrative partner but as an Assistant Principal who will promptly take care of the endless administrative minutia.

I typed in her name in the Google search box, pressed Enter and waited. A list of search results appeared on screen. As the full significance of the words registered in my consciousness, I could feel my heartbeat rapidly increase. Search results:

- *SoHo Principal's 'voodoo' backfires as she is removed from Terrace High School.*
- *Principal to be fired over school ritual.*
- *Exorcise class.*
- *Principal brings in Santeria priestess to drive away bad spirits.*
- *Downtown Principal removed after Santeria ceremony.*
- *'Charm' School 'Voodoo' Principal Axed for Spell-ing.*

I cannot recall how many times I reread these headlines. It would be an understatement to say that the immediate impact of what I read totally threw me for a loop. A thousand and one speeding thoughts swirled, careening inside my head like high speed bumper cars with such velocity that my head spun.

When the 'Voodoo Principal' news item hit the newspapers in the summer of 2007, I had just completed my twenty-third year with the New

York City Department of Education and my first year at Terrace High School. A Math teacher from another Manhattan high school was installed as the new principal. I stayed on to support him for three years before sailing off into the sunset.

ABOUT THE AUTHOR

With an undergraduate degree in French from St. Francis College, Brooklyn, and two graduate degrees in Education from Teachers College, Columbia University, Ira Sumner Simmonds has worked as House Manager at Alice Tully Hall, Lincoln Center for the Performing Arts, Inc., and spent twenty-six years as a teacher and administrator in New York City Public Schools. He currently works as an educational consultant.